Faith Never SHRINKS in Hot Water

To Lynn —
Blessings
Linda
Shepherd

Faith Never SHRINKS in Hot Water

by

Linda Shepherd

Pacific Press Publishing
Nampa, Idaho
Oshawa, Ontario, Canada

Edited by Bonnie Tyson-Flyn
Cover illustration by Susan Gal
Cover and inside design by Michelle Petz
Typeset in 13/15 Bernhard Modern.

All scriptures are from the New International Version unless otherwise stated.

Shepherd, Linda E., 1957-
    Faith Never shrinks in hot water : inspirational
stories for women who want their faith to grow / Linda
Shepherd.
        p.   cm.
    ISBN 0-8163-1326-1 (pbk. : alk. paper)
    1. Women—Prayer-books and devotions—English.
2. Christian life—Meditations.   I. Title.
BV4844.S533 1996
242'.643—dc20   96-33832
                                                CIP

96 97 98 99 00 • 5 4 3 2 1

Contents

Dedication

Thank You, Lord, for seeing me through such tough times. Thank You for all Your love and blessings. Thank You for giving me such a wonderful husband and children. You are my everything.

Thank you Paul, for being a faithful husband. Thank you for your support and encouragement. I love you very much.

Thank you, Laura and Jimmy, for being such wonderful kids. You have taught me so much. You have given me joy and made my life very rich. Thank you for letting me share your stories.

Flashlight Walk

1

The hot June day had cooled under a starless Texas sky. Crickets chirped and a soft breeze rocked the branches of the shadowy live oaks outside the farmhouse.

Jimmy and I had planned to walk down to Grandpop's and Grandmop's mailbox all afternoon, but the sticky, breath-stealing heat had kept us trying to keep cool by the kitchen fan.

Now the rustle of evening breezes swayed the tall grasses, and the sunset faded to black. Jimmy found a flashlight and turned its yellow beam toward a window that framed the darkness. The flashlight's beam reflected a dot of yellow light on the glass.

"Let's take our walk, now!" my five-year-old suggested. "This flashlight will help us see where to go."

We slipped into an evening waiting for the moonrise still to come. The light from Jimmy's flashlight pooled into halos across our dark path. Jimmy hummed a tuneless song while I swatted at a mosquito buzzing near my ear.

We held hands, my feet falling in rhythm with Jimmy's. My steps just touched the hem of the flashlight's glowing beam gliding silently before us.

A dog barked somewhere in the darkness, and the beam bounced off the path and disappeared into the cow pasture.

My feet continued to fall where I hoped the path lay. But I felt disoriented in the blackness. The memory of a twilight encounter with a slithering copperhead sparked me to comment, "Shine the light on the path, Jimmy."

Again, the light bounced at my feet. *Ah, no snakes—just solid ground*, I thought as I walked on in the orb that lighted my path, one step at a time.

A live oak's leaves trembled as a gust of wind skimmed past. "What was that?" Jimmy asked, pointing the flashlight beam into the tree.

My feet patted the darkness as my guiding light danced above my head. "Just the wind. Shine the light on the path," I suggested again. "I can't see where I'm going."

The light swept from the tree and onto my feet. Again I felt assurance as my tennis shoes trod the illuminated path.

"Jimmy, did you know God's Word is like this flashlight?"

"How's that, Mommy?"

"Psalm 119:105 says,

*'Your word is a lamp to my feet
and a light for my path.' "*

"What does that mean?"

"As long as we follow God's teachings, we will not trip. We will know where to go—one step at a time. It's just like this flashlight beam. As long as it's pointed at the ground, we know we won't fall, get lost, or step on a snake."

At the mention of snakes, Jimmy's bouncing beam held steady.

"Jimmy, why don't you try turning the light off for a second?"

Blackness engulfed us.

"I feel lost!" Jimmy said, flipping the light back on. The beam illuminated our pebbled path. "But I can see where to go now!" he said.

"It's the same with God's Word. If we know what it says, we won't get lost. We will be able to see where to go with our lives."

Later, as I thought about our evening walk, I remembered a discussion I had had with a friend.

"Linda, don't worry so much about the direction God wants you to take with your life," Ellen had advised. "He's probably not going to reveal all the details now, but watch—He will guide you, one step at a time."

As I think back over the way I have traveled, I am glad God did not reveal too much of my journey too soon. If I had known, for instance, my daughter's future when she was only a newborn, I would have been swallowed by premature grief.

Faith Never Shrinks in Hot Water

How great it is to know God is in charge of illuminating the dark pathway my life must travel. His Word and guidance will light each step I take. His illumination never reaches farther than I need to see, yet I know He will never leave me in the dark.

Parachute Answers

2

I used to think God was sometimes far away from me when I needed Him most. But my then three-year-old helped me to change this belief.

Whenever we drove near the Loveland airport, Jimmy would often spy the silhouette of a parachutist floating to the ground. I had no idea what an impression this had on him until we drove by the scattered wreckage of a car crash. Lights flashed and emergency personnel shuttled victims into waiting ambulances.

The sight of crumpled vehicles caused my mind to flash back to the afternoon several years before when my own car had crashed. I remembered hunching over my young daughter, who had been thrown into the freeway, still strapped in her car seat. I remembered wondering if she would live or die as I screamed for help. The answering sirens shifted my thoughts to the present, and my voice jolted to prayer.

"Jesus," I called as I slowed my van to a traffic-jam crawl, "those people being loaded into the ambulances need Your help! Don't let them die. Show them how much You love them."

I was startled when Jimmy shouted a prayer of his own. "Jesus!" he called. "Help those people! Put on Your parachute and get down here!"

At first, I felt compelled to explain Jesus didn't wear a parachute. But as I thought about it, the more tangible Jimmy's picture of Jesus seemed. As I looked skyward, I could almost picture Jesus and a multitude of angels gliding toward the rescue operation on the wings of heavenly silk.

Suddenly, the memory of my own tragedy changed. Instead of seeing myself alone on the side of the highway, crying over the limp body of my injured daughter, I pictured Jesus by my side. At the time of the accident, I was unaware of His presence. But as I replayed the scene in my mind, I could almost feel His arm around my shoulders. I could imagine His compassionate face as I cried out to Him for help.

This new perspective of my own tragedy caused me to wonder if my son's idea of Jesus floating down from the heavens was, in fact, more real than my idea that Jesus had been removed from my hurt and pain. After all, King David said,

"The Lord is near to those who have a broken heart"
(Psalm 34:18, NKJV).

So although Jesus hadn't really worn a parachute the day of our accident, He had really brought me comfort and healing. And over time, He had turned my tragedy into triumph and my sorrow into joy.

Since the afternoon of Jimmy's parachute prayer, I look up when things look grim, expecting to see a heavenly parachute floating in my direction.

After all, while I waited ten months for my daughter, Laura, to awaken from her coma following our car crash, I was never alone. He was with me, even when I did not recognize His presence.

How Big Is God?

Have you ever wondered how big God is? Have you ever tried to describe His glory?

Recently, I tried to explain God's greatness to a kindergarten Sunday School class. First I read my poem, "Paul's Cotton":

Once, a young boy named Paul,
Couldn't hear God at all.
With his ears full of cotton—
He thought he was forgotten—
Though God knocked and He phoned and He called.

When I finished reading, I asked, "What do you suppose this poem means?"

A freckle-faced girl spoke up, her eyes bright under a pink hair ribbon. "We can't hear God if we've got cotton in our ears."

"We need to listen to God," a suit-clad boy responded.

"If we listen for God's voice, what do you suppose He would say?" I asked.

The children shook their heads.

"He would tell you He loves you," I answered.

All the children smiled, except a blond boy named Jon. He scowled thoughtfully, then raised his hand. "How big is God?" he asked.

"He's as big as you can imagine—and then bigger."

The boy in the suit asked, "Is He as big as a camel?"

"Yes. God is bigger than a camel. He created camels," I replied.

Jon folded his arms across his red sweater. "Is He bigger than a giraffe?"

"Yes. God created giraffes."

In frustration, Jon asked, "Is He bigger than the whole world?"

"Yes," I laughed. "God created the world. In fact, He created the universe. King David said in Psalm 145:3,

> *'Great is the Lord and most worthy of praise;*
> *his greatness no one can fathom.' "*

Jon tossed his hands into the air. "Then how can God fit into my heart?"

My eyebrows rose. "That's a hard one, but let me ask you

a question." I leaned forward. "How big is your love for your mom and dad?"

Jon held his hands about a foot apart. "About this big."

"But," I responded, "your heart is smaller than that. How can you fit all that love in there?"

Jon looked puzzled. "I don't know."

I leaned forward, my eyes holding his gaze. "The way God fits into our hearts is the same way the love for our moms and dads fits into our hearts. It's hard to understand now, but the important thing is to ask God to come into your heart. He'll find room to grow, and He will fill your heart with a love for Him."

Bitter Lesson 4

"I hate Jordan," three-year-old Jimmy cried. "He hit me. I'll never forgive him."

Jimmy and I were standing outside the church under a blanket of stars. As I looked down at my pint-sized volcano, I was stung by his sense of outrage.

"Jimmy," I cooed, "you may be angry at Jordan now, but you'll get over it."

"No, I won't. I hate him. He hurt me," Jimmy answered, clenching his fist.

I looked heavenward, wondering how to handle this childish display of venom. After all, the venom didn't hurt three-year-old Jordan; it poisoned only my son.

No wonder Jesus commanded us to forgive others, I realized. *Bitterness affects the grudge bearer—not the person who wronged him or her.*

Again, I tried to soften Jimmy's anger. "Jimmy, you've got to forgive Jordan. That's what Jesus would want you to do."

"Never!" he shouted, tears streaming down his cheeks. "I'll never forgive him."

I thought of the words of Matthew 6:14, 15,

> *"If you forgive men when they sin against you,*
> *your heavenly Father will also forgive you.*
> *But if you do not forgive men their sins,*
> *your Father will not forgive your sins."*

I had never quite understood why Jesus was so harsh in this area. But now, as I saw unforgiveness seething in my three-year-old, I made a discovery. God doesn't want us to forgive others because they need to be freed from our wrath. Rather, God wants us to forgive others because *we* need to be freed from our own bitterness.

Taking a risk, I said, "All right, Jimmy. You don't have to forgive Jordan. But if you won't, I won't be able to forgive you."

Jimmy quickly turned his face up to mine. "I forgive him, Mommy," he said, unwilling to forego my affection. His anger melted, and he smiled through his tears.

I gave him a hug. "I forgive you too." I smiled up at the night stars, grateful I had a God wise enough to motivate me to forgive others too.

The Journey Starts

Covering my eyes with my hands, I tried to block the horror of the afternoon as I huddled beside the emergency-room hallway window. A storm raged outside the hospital; another storm raged within my heart. The more I tried to forget, the more clearly I could see myself behind the wheel of my car.

The scene swirled through my thoughts: eighteen-month-old Laura snuggling into her car seat—the red taillights reflecting on the damp pavement—my foot reaching for the brakes—my car lurching across the dividing line—the accelerating minivan. . . .

Then the thunderous explosion of metal ripping through

metal roared in my ears as my body strained against the seat belt. The silence that followed chilled my heart. Why, why wasn't my baby crying?

I turned to the back seat, expecting to look into Laura's frightened, blue-gray eyes. Instead, I stared into a jagged, twisted hole.

Unlatching my seat belt, I clawed my way through the wreckage. I feared finding Laura's body in the crumpled debris. Instead, I found her in the middle of the freeway, still fastened in her car seat, dazed and still.

A doctor rushed past me, slamming the heavy emergency-room doors. Back to the present, I lifted my head, watching the staff's continued fight for Laura's life. *Jesus, help them!* I pleaded.

Soon I was ushered into the hospital waiting room.

When my husband, Paul, arrived, he was damp with rain and tears. I rushed into his arms.

"Is—is she going to be OK?" he asked.

"I don't know," I choked. "She has a fractured skull."

We sat together, silently, staring at the floor, our voices stolen by shock and grief.

The days that followed the car accident were critical as Laura fought for her life. Each time Laura thrashed with seizures, her nurses rushed her to X-ray, and I stumbled behind, blinded by grief.

Each CAT scan sent Laura back into surgery to relieve the pressure building in her brain. "We're sorry," the doctor finally said, "but Laura will never awaken. She's in a vegetative state."

As only a mother could know, I knew Laura was not a

vegetable but a little girl held captive by her body. Looking at my sleeping beauty, I constantly cried, *How much longer, God?*

Days turned into months. One evening, a physician stood in the doorway of Laura's hospital room, listening to the mechanical breathing of Laura's respirator. He avoided my eyes as his words chilled the air. "Linda, Laura is not going to recover—you might as well—"

His unspoken words screamed, "End it now! Pull the plug!" He awaited my response. I swallowed hard, knowing we were playing a dangerous game, a game Laura couldn't afford for me to lose. I wearily tried to hide in silence, wishing for the deadly moment to pass. Finally, I found my voice. "But my daughter is not dead!" I announced, fighting to sound calm.

To avoid an emotional outburst that would give the doctor control, I took a deep breath and clenched my fists. "Laura—Laura has too much brain activity! Besides, what makes you think she's not going to recover?"

The doctor led me into a nearby office. "You need to face facts. Half of Laura's brain has been destroyed."

"But half of her brain is intact. Are you telling me you can scientifically factor the impact my love, faith, and prayers will have on this child's future?"

"No," the doctor grudgingly admitted.

I pressed. "Then your prognosis is only a guess. You see, God can take Laura, if He decides that is best. He has my permission. But it is not my role to pull her plug!"

The doctor sighed, realizing Laura would live. He rose, and I followed him out of his office. Moments later, I leaned against the doorjamb to Laura's room and closed my eyes, trying to still my rapid heartbeat.

This victory is won, but how many other battles are left to fight? I wondered. I thought of Psalm 23:4:

> *"Even though I walk through the valley of the shadow
> of death, I will fear no evil, for you are with me;
> your rod and your staff, they comfort me."*

Lord, I prayed, *please see me through. For my hope and comfort are in You and You alone.*

The Wall

Have you ever wondered why some people seem walled away from God? I have. This worry prompted me, my junior year in high school, to join thirty other teens from my church's youth group on a trip to Galveston Island to tell tourists about Jesus.

My first experience sharing my faith made me nervous. Who did I think I was, anyway? These tourists were here to relax, not to think about their ultimate destinies. But my anxiety was soon lulled by the waves rolling onto the beach below and by the blue sky stretching above. As I relaxed, I began to see myself as a champion of the gospel, ready to handle any crisis that came my way.

Walking past a seashell shop, my partner, Stephanie, and I discovered two hiding co-workers. One look at Elaine and Carol told us something had gone wrong.

"What's the matter?" I asked.

Carol held back tears. "We were handing out tracts when we ran into a man who asked a question we couldn't answer."

"What did he ask?" I demanded.

"He wanted to know whether God was so great that He could make a wall so strong that even He couldn't break it?"

"Of course!" I interrupted, eager to defend my faith—a faith I had not yet tested.

"That's what we said," Carol injected, allowing her blond hair to hide her sad eyes. "Then he asked, 'If God's so great, why couldn't He get past the wall?' "

"Oh!" I responded, deflating like a punctured balloon. "A trick question."

I turned to walk the sea wall, wondering whether the question was really a trick or if my faith, which I had inherited from my parents, was flawed. Searching for answers, I gazed into the horizon and prayed, *Lord, help me understand*.

A sentence from Psalm 69:32 drifted into my thoughts:

"You who seek God, your hearts shall live" (NKJV).

The solution startled me—it was almost too simple.

I hurried to the seashell shop, where my friends still huddled.

"I found the answer!" I gasped.

Stephanie's, Carol's, and Elaine's forlorn eyes widened. "Really?"

"God has already created a wall like that man described—it's the human heart," I explained. "Although God is mighty enough, He'll never break through the wall. God will enter only if we invite Him in."

Hang-ups!

I constantly experiment with techniques to get phone solicitors off the line. I try to be gentle and firm and yet get through the interruption and go about my business as quickly as possible.

The only salespeople I ever listen to are the ones who sound as if they might jump off a bridge if I refuse their call. Yet if I let them, these emotionally fragile callers will demand my ear for fifteen to twenty minutes as they laboriously read a sales transcript. YUCK!

But the phone calls I hate the most are the aggressive solicitors. These callers will not let me off the hook—graciously.

RING RING!

"Good morning, I'm from Awacko's Aluminum Siding."

"I'm not interested in aluminum siding," I explain sweetly. "I live in an all-brick house."

"Oh, that makes no difference. You see, our product has a special built-in mosquito repellent. Brick or no brick, you'll want—"

I interrupt. "Really, I don't—"

"Ah, did I tell you it glows in the dark? A lovely shade of lime green! Your visitors can always find where you live, even on the darkest, snowiest of nights!"

"Yes, but—"

"Our workers will be at your house at five in the morning to start work—"

"No, I don't think—"

"If I can just confirm your address and your charge-card number—now, what did you say your card's expiration date is?"

CLICK.

Let's face it, there are some calls you just have to hang up on, unless you want to buy a product you don't want, you like being scammed, or you don't mind obscene phone calls.

The last obscene caller who dialed my number actually hung up on me. It seems he didn't like the scriptures I read to him. I still think John 3:16 was an appropriate passage.

The worst series of calls I ever received came early one afternoon. Mason Summer, a nineteen-year-old friend, phoned, very upset.

"Linda, I just got a phone call from someone who says I bought a ribbon watch—whatever that is! And he said I owe his company five hundred dollars. He also says that if I don't give him my charge-card number within the next two hours, he's going to turn the case over to an attorney, which will cost me an additional five hundred dollars!"

"Have you talked to your mom or dad about this?" I asked.

"They're not home. And I don't know where they are. The problem is, this man says I have to give him my charge-card number NOW!"

I said, "Well, hold on just a minute. The last thing I want you to do is to give this stranger access to your credit-card account. Do you have a phone number for this guy?" I asked.

"Yes, I'm supposed to call him back."

"Give the number to me. I'll take care of him."

A man answered on the first ring. "I'm glad you called on Mason's behalf," he said. "Now, if you will just give me your charge-card number, we can clear this matter up."

"Wait just a minute!" I injected. "Let's get this straight. Mason claims he has not purchased a watch from your company."

The voice on the other end of the line sighed. "That's what all these young people say," he replied. "They get themselves into a little financial trouble; then they claim they never made the purchase."

"Not Mason," I explained. "He wouldn't do that. If he says he did not purchase a watch, I believe him."

"Now," the man drawled, "You can easily clear this up later. But first, give me your charge-card number and pay the debt. Then you can call the company and get a refund."

I laughed. "If you think I am going to give you my charge-card number, you are mistaken. I don't know who you are! I don't know if you are really who you claim to be. For all I know, this is a credit-card scam!"

The would-be bill collector's demeanor changed. After calling me a few names, he hung up.

I felt bewildered. But I didn't have to feel that way for long. The collector called right back and spoke to me as if I were his best friend.

"Sir, I'll make a deal with you," I replied. "Give me the name and number of the company you are collecting for, and I will call to verify the bill."

He did. And as it turned out, I uncovered a case of mistaken identity. A ribbon watch had indeed been purchased by a Mason Summer, but a different Mason Summer—a Mason who lived across town from my friend Mason.

And I found out that the bill collector was very aware my friend Mason was most likely not the Mason he was looking for, but what did he care? He only wanted to collect the bill, from whatever Mason, Linda, Tom, Dick, or Harry he could find.

Jesus said in Matthew 10:16,

"I am sending you out like sheep among wolves.
Therefore be as shrewd as snakes
and as innocent as doves."

This is good advice for many occasions in life. The next time a phone solicitor annoys you, find a way to hang up graciously. And whatever you do, be WISE—don't give out your charge-card number on any account!

The Gift

I sat in the stillness of my twenty-one-month-old daughter's hospital room, holding her hand, watching for signs of life. As I studied her, Laura looked as if her dark lashes would flutter open and she would sit up, ending our almost-two-month-long nightmare.

How I longed to hear Laura's giggle as she snuggled with her silky hair against my cheek while I read to her from one of her favorite books.

Impulsively, I leaned over and kissed her cherubic face. "Honey, it's Mommy. I love you. I know you're in there. I'm waiting—"

The words caught in my throat, and I shut my eyes. If

only I could turn back the hand of time and avoid the collision that had saturated our lives with grief.

I remembered sitting in the emergency-room waiting room with my husband, tearfully waiting for the doctor's verdict.

Paul and I hugged each other and shouted with joy when the doctor told us, "Laura's going to be all right. Now go home and get some rest."

But as I lay my head on my pillow, my dreams spun out of control. I woke up in a cold sweat, picturing the blood that had trickled out of Laura's ear. *Laura is not OK. The crash was too violent. I have to get back to the hospital!*

I raced my car through the rain-slicked, predawn streets. Once in Laura's ICU room, I found the staff gathered around her body as it quaked with convulsions.

God, where are You? I cried like the psalmist.

Three months later, Laura had been moved to another hospital, where she still remained unresponsive. I continued to cry, *Lord, when will You answer my call?*

One evening, as I sat by her bed, listening to the mechanical breathing of her respirator, a strange mood of uncertainty settled over me. I looked at the child I had fought and prayed so hard to keep. *She's really in there, isn't she?*

I stood up, trying to shake the doubt that had suddenly caught me off guard. Noticing that my watch read 11:00, I decided to get ready for bed. Because my husband, Paul, was out of town, I wouldn't drive home but would sleep in Laura's room. Flipping off the light, I shut the door. The nurses had already completed their evening rounds. It would be hours before anyone would check on us. I felt alone, too alone. I popped two extra-strength pain relievers and set the bottle on a nearby tray table beside my glass of water. *What if the doctors are right—and Laura never wakes up?* I thought as I spread a blanket in the window seat.

Fluffing my pillow, I wondered about God. *Maybe He's abandoned us. Maybe He isn't going to answer my prayers. Just who am I trying to fool?* I questioned. *I need to face facts: Laura will never awaken. She'll live the rest of her life as a vegetable, hooked to life support.*

I tried to stifle my despair, but Laura's respirator seemed to rhythmically mock, *no-hope, no-hope, no-hope.* My chest constricted. Everything suddenly seemed so different, so pointless. *Laura would be better off if she were to die,* I concluded. *After all, I can't allow her to live in this suspended state of life, can I?*

I couldn't bear to ask the doctors to take my child off life support after I had already prevented this action once before. But now, I accepted that Laura's smile would never return. My dreams for her life were dashed. And God? He had been as silent as Laura's stilled voice.

I was truly alone—miles from my husband, miles from Laura's awareness, and light-years from the God I had trusted.

Perhaps God's silence meant I needed to take matters into my own hands. Perhaps it was up to me to end this horrible suffering.

I can kill Laura without the doctor's help, I reasoned. *I can turn off the alarms and unplug the respirator from the wall. It would be so simple, except—except,* I wondered, *if I kill my daughter, how can I live with myself? How can I face Paul or my parents?*

I found myself staring at my bottle of painkillers. My Tylenol! *If I swallowed them . . . no one would find us until morning. . . . Laura and I could . . . escape . . . this living hell . . . together.*

Just as my plan seemed like the only solution, I found my hand resting on my belly. My hidden child was only two weeks old, but I knew he was there.

My mind slowly cleared. How could I kill myself? How could I kill Laura? A new life was growing inside me. A life that had the right to live!

My perspective returned. *Lord, I'm willing to wait—despite the pain and the cost. I'm willing to wait on You.*

The word *wait* brought Isaiah 40:31 into my consciousness.

"They that wait upon the Lord shall renew their strength; they shall mount up with wings as eagles; they shall run, and not be weary; and they shall walk, and not faint" (KJV).

I cried myself to sleep, terrified of the future, terrified of the murders I had almost committed.

Nine months later, my daughter began to emerge from her coma just before her baby brother, Jimmy, was born.

Although her eyes fluttered open, her gaze was fixed. She remained hooked to life support and slumped in her wheelchair, totally paralyzed. But though she was diagnosed as blind, her eyes began to focus once again. Laura began to greet us with a cheerful "Hi!"

Although I still sometimes weep over the Laura I have

35

lost, I embrace the Laura who has returned. Recently, when she and Jimmy were baptized, at their requests, the tears in my eyes were not from sorrow, but from joy. How glad I am that I waited on God instead of going through with my murderous midnight plan.

I still face obstacles. But God enables me to run the race set before me. A race I now know I can finish.

Faith Walk

Recently, I heard a speaker talk of the cruelty our country's white forebears inflicted on their black brothers and sisters. As she talked, I felt my cheeks burn. My great-great-greats eight generations back were slave owners from the South. But these people seemed so far removed from me. Was I still connected to their long-ago injustices?

I stung with shame as I listened to the speaker list their crimes. I felt sorry to somehow be connected with these stories of oppression.

When the congregation bowed their heads in prayer, I asked the Lord, *But what can I do now? I'm not responsible for my ancestors' actions, am I?*

Feeling justified, I concluded my prayer and raised my head. That's when my heavenly Father guided my attention to a black woman, dressed in a pale green suit, sitting near me. *Apologize to her*, He directed.

But this woman and my ancestors are strangers to me, I argued. *Am I responsible for what took place over a century ago?*

Apologize anyway, God seemed to say.

After the service, I stalked my unsuspecting sister. I trembled with relief when she didn't notice me. After all, what was I supposed to say to her? My ancestors owned slaves, and I'm sorry! She'd probably spit in my eye, I decided. Yet, the call to love my neighbor had been too strong to ignore. For as 1 John 4:20 says,

"If someone says, 'I love God,' and hates his brother, he is a liar; for he who does not love his brother whom he has seen, how can he love God whom he has not seen?" (NKJV).

Somehow, I had to let my sister know I loved her. I followed her to the book table and watched her browse. I noticed her grimace as she searched her purse. Her expression told me she had forgotten her checkbook. As she turned to leave, I grabbed my opportunity and purchased the book she had wanted. Quickly, I followed her to the other side of the auditorium.

Feeling like a fool, I thrust the book at her. "Pardon me, but I want to give this to you."

Her brown eyes widened, and she looked into my face.

"The Lord spoke to me and told me to apologize to you," I continued, knowing she'd either reject me or think I was some kind of loony tune.

Her eyes held steady. "Apologize, why?"

Blushing with shame, I explained, "You see, my ancestors owned slaves. I'm really sorry. I'm impressed that the Lord wants you to know how I feel. Will you forgive me?"

Her eyes filled with tears, and she surrounded me with her arms. "I do forgive you," she cried.

After our tearful hug, she looked at me and smiled. "I'm so glad I came to church today. I almost stayed home, but the Lord told me that if I came, He would do something special for me—and He has. He sent you."

I smiled, too, relieved by her acceptance and excited to know that I had heard God's voice.

But the most amazing thing was that in my obedience to God's promptings, I received a gift too. I made a new friend.

Red Mole Warning

I worry about my husband, Paul, a lot. After all, he is the king of the mountains. Really! He's climbed all fifty-four of Colorado's fourteen-thousand-foot peaks. Even when we lived in Texas, Paul would find a way to escape to Colorado for a little back-country adventure.

Once he talked me into climbing Colorado's fourteen-thousand-foot Mount Baldy with him. It was the most terrifying experience of my life! Even though the mountain is what most mountaineers call a "walk-up," I felt terrified by its sheer steepness. "If I slipped," I commented, staring down a grassy slope that seemed almost vertical, "I would fall forever."

I'm happy to say, I didn't fall. And after scrambling over the boulder field at the top, I didn't even come home with any bruises.

But even with all his mountaineering experience, there is one thing Paul almost never fails to bring home from the mountains—and that's a deep red sunburn.

Despite my nagging, Paul somehow forgets to douse himself with his sunblock 45. Because of his sunburning history, I watch him closely for any unusual skin changes.

Recently, Paul and I were eating dinner in a dimly lighted Chinese restaurant when I first noticed it. There was a bright red mole on his cheek. Paul had always had a mole on that cheek, but it had never been bright red.

I took his hand and warned him, "Paul, you have to go to the skin doctor first thing Monday morning. You have a mole that's turning red."

Paul quietly agreed. It wasn't until later that night we discussed it again. The lights were off when he crawled into bed. His voice was low and serious. "Linda?" he said. "You know that red mole on my cheek?"

"Yes. You have to go see the doctor about it, Monday and no later."

"The mole's not there anymore."

I propped myself up on one elbow. "What do you mean?"

"I was just looking at it in the bathroom mirror, and I pulled it off."

I sat up in bed, my heart pounding. "WHAT?"

"Don't worry."

"Paul, you don't just pull moles off your face—especially suspicious-looking ones!"

"It wasn't a mole," he replied.

"Then what was it?"

He couldn't stifle a chuckle. "It was a crushed red pepper."

I flopped back onto the pillow. "You're kidding!"

"Nope. I guess I'd worn it since lunch."

As my heartrate began to normalize, I clobbered Paul with my pillow. "That's for scaring me half to death!" I laughed.

Paul gave me a false alarm with that red pepper. But even so, I will continue to watch his skin carefully. I like having him around, even though he doesn't fight fair when the pillows are flying. Besides, I am his helper. As Genesis 2:18 points out,

"The Lord God said, 'It is not good for the man to be alone. I will make a helper suitable for him.' "

So when Paul sometimes tires of my "advice," I remind him that I'm his God-given helper and that I'm only doing my job—helping the man I love.

Letters to Death Row

"Linda," my mother's voice crackled across the phone line. "Sharon Cain* disappeared last weekend!"

I felt a sudden sickness in the pit of my stomach. Sharon wasn't a close friend, but I knew her well enough to be concerned. "You're kidding!" I said. "I saw Sharon Saturday. What happened?"

My mother paused. "That's the day she was reported missing. Apparently, she and her husband were walking home from the Gateway Shopping Center after their car broke down."

I sat down, overwhelmed. "That's where I saw her," I stammered. "It—it never occurred to me that she needed help. I thought she and her husband were heading for a nearby restaurant!"

My mother continued to update me as news reports drifted in. Shortly after I had seen them, Sharon's husband had sprinted ahead, planning to return for his wife with their other car. Meanwhile, a stranger accelerated down the road toward Sharon. When he saw her walking alone, he screeched to a halt, swung open the car door, and yanked her inside. Then he drove to an isolated beach on the Texas Gulf Coast. After brutalizing her, he abandoned her—leaving her to die, buried alive in the sand.

Over the next few days, the ugly facts played over and over in my mind. The more I thought about them, the more furious I became with myself for not stopping to see why they were on foot. God had put them directly in my path, and I had blown it.

I didn't know! I argued with my conscience. *I couldn't have known Sharon was in danger.* In a sense, I was also a victim of this senseless tragedy.

I spent the next few nights in sleeplessness, turning the blame and anger from myself to Sharon's murderer. Months later, when Thomas Wilson* was tried and sentenced to die by electrocution, I was elated. I believed that even hell was too good for this man. Over time, my bitterness only intensified.

But then one morning during church, I listened as our silver-haired pastor spoke from Mark 11:25:

"When you stand praying, if you hold anything against anyone, forgive him, so that your Father in heaven may forgive you your sins."

This message shocked me. *This can't possibly apply to me and my hatred for Sharon's killer, can it, Lord?* But I already knew the answer. *It isn't fair!* I silently screamed. *That man had no right to rob Sharon of her life! I can't believe You would want me to forgive him after what he did!*

I wrestled silently for months, contemplating the monstrous wrong committed against Sharon, her friends, and her family. I even mourned for the children she would never bear. Thomas Wilson's actions were unjustifiable, and therefore, I concluded, unforgivable.

As I sat on my sofa one evening, a question came to mind: To receive God's forgiveness, must one's sin always be accompanied by a good excuse? I opened my Bible to Romans 3:23, 24:

"All have sinned and fall short of the glory of God, and are justified freely by his grace through the redemption that came by Christ Jesus."

According to that passage, God's forgiveness is given freely, no matter the circumstances.

In one painful moment, I knew I had to forgive Thomas Wilson—regardless of his crime—excuse or no excuse.

My heart rebelled as my mind made a decision. It would be hard to give up my hatred, like exchanging a custom-fitted garment for one much too big. Even so, I weakly told the Lord that with His help, I was willing to try to forgive this man, though it seemed far beyond my ability.

My first problem was how. How does one go about forgiving the unforgivable? And how would I know if I had succeeded? Though several years had passed, the mere mention of Thomas Wilson's name still sent shivers down my spine.

But before I took any action, I received word that Thomas Wilson had been executed. I couldn't help but feel relief that this episode of my life had ended. Or so I thought.

One day while reading in the sunlit bay window of my new home, I saw an item about an organization called Death Row Support Project. I began to feel the Lord prompting me to test my so-called forgiveness on a real person.

"Don't do it, Linda," my mother cautioned. "Think of the victims' families."

"I sympathize with them," I agreed. "But I have to find out how big God's forgiveness really is."

After much trepidation and a few crumpled starts, I wrote a letter, asking the project to send me the name of a death-row inmate with whom I could correspond. I secretly hoped I would get the name of someone whose crime would be easy to forgive.

When the letter arrived from the project, I opened it with trembling hands. I was shocked to read that the organization had sent me the name of Johnny Lee Simpson,* a convicted murderer from my own hometown of Beaumont, Texas.

My mother was horrified. "He killed two women during a bank robbery! First, he shared a cup of coffee with them; then he shot each of them in the head!"

Pregnant with my first child, I, too, was appalled this man had killed two young mothers.

With difficulty, I began writing to Johnny. And the sensitive replies that came from this intelligent fifty-year-old convict amazed me.

"Who would have thought my life would have turned out like this?" Johnny wrote. "There was a time when I taught a boys' Sunday School class. But I've turned my back on all that. Don't pity me. I've made my own choices. I want to die to pay the debt I owe society."

Through our correspondence, Johnny shared in my joy over the birth of my daughter, Laura, and grieved with me when she was injured in our terrible car crash. "I sat up all night in my cell and thought solely of Laura and you in that hospital. Before daylight, I got the definite feeling that Laura was going to be fine and would grow into a lovely woman. You are not alone."

Somehow, it was easier for me to forgive Johnny, not because he deserved it, but because God's hand was moving in our lives. I could feel God's love and compassion for him, just as he had felt God's love and compassion for us.

One March morning, Johnny sent bad news: "An hour ago, I received another date of execution—May 3. As I have turned my back on my own faith, I shall not be a hypocrite and ask for God's forgiveness. Please understand."

"But, Johnny," I wrote in my next letter, "none of us deserve God's forgiveness. Can't you see that God will look past your sins, if you only ask?"

His letter was a blow. "Many long and lost years ago I had a deep and abiding faith, which I alone destroyed. In so doing, I destroyed myself. I cannot look back. I will die without God."

With Johnny's execution date only weeks away, I yearned to see him experience God's redeeming power. If only I could help him understand!

As I sat at my typewriter, trying to define God's forgiveness for Johnny in story form, the enormity of His grace and mercy became real to me. With great anticipation and prayer, I mailed my letter and waited for a response.

It never came. Instead, God revealed His grace to Johnny without my help.

"Very late Thursday night," Johnny wrote, "I had my back turned to the bars . . . listening to all the yelling and cussing, but suddenly, I did not hear a sound, only a voice within me saying, 'You shall not die; there are things you have to do.'

"Later, my Bible dropped from the shelf onto my bunk. I picked it up, and it fell open to Colossians 1:13, 14: 'He has rescued us from the dominion of darkness and brought us into the kingdom of the Son he loves, in whom we have redemption, the forgiveness of sins.'

"I understand now. Jesus has forgiven even me, even though I don't deserve it. I'm part of His kingdom now."

I read the letter with joy, realizing that in the process of becoming Johnny's friend, the Lord had totally removed the last traces of bitterness from my spirit over the murder of my friend, Sharon. I was wonderfully free!

And Johnny? Today, after a year of leading a Bible study in his cell block and writing letters to children on a hospital cancer ward, he faced his final execution date. Someday, when I meet Johnny in heaven, I will give him a great big hug. I'll probably even say, "I told you so.

*The names have been changed to protect the victims and their families.

Lost Hope

In the years since the accident, Laura turned into a happy little girl. But still I struggled with the belief that if my faith were strong enough, Laura could be healed.

One rainy afternoon a couple of years after the accident, I slipped into Laura's room, armed with my Bible, praise tapes, and carefully written "faith" statements that described my goal that God would soon heal my daughter's disabilities.

I had looked forward to this afternoon for days—a rare opportunity for Laura and me to be alone. I planned to spend our time together with God, proving by my prayers, songs, and statements that I had enough faith to see Laura arise and walk.

4—F.N.S.H.W.

But after an hour of earnestly telling God how much I believed that He would perform a miraculous healing, I hit a wall. Suddenly, I knew that my three-year struggle to carefully craft my faith had been for nothing. I discovered that I had no more strength left to believe. I had fought with all my might—and I had lost.

I kissed Laura's white cheek and watched her eyelashes flutter open as she fixed her gaze upon the ceiling as if I were not there. The lump that had been in my throat suddenly knotted in my stomach. I tried to continue, turning the onion-skinned pages of my Bible to yet another "faith" Scripture. But the suddenly blurry print could not give me hope. Sighing, I shut the Book.

Laura's never going to get better, I anguished as the rain pattered against Laura's windowpane, saturating my spirit with despair. *Our situation is hopeless.*

Later, I hid in the darkness of my bedroom, curtains drawn against the cold drizzle. I realized that my hope was lost, replaced with shattered dreams. *Lord*, I prayed, *are You there? I need You to speak to me, if You want me to continue in my hope. Please show me what to do.*

That evening in church, the thundering voice of my pastor dropped to a low rumble. "The Lord has impressed me that there is someone here tonight who has lost hope."

I froze in amazement as goose bumps crawled up my arms.

The pastor's eyes searched the congregation of hundreds, as I tried to appear invisible. "God wants you to look up. He is with you and will restore your hope in Him."

I was stunned. This message was too immediate to be a coincidence. *Maybe God is with me*, I reasoned.

Driving home after the meeting, I turned my attention from myself to God. I began to see I had missed God's truth by placing my faith, not in Him, but in an earthly vessel—me. I had spent all of my energy trying to have faith in my faith! Like two index fingers trapped by their struggle against the woven fibers of a Chinese finger puzzle, I had been held captive by trusting myself instead of trusting God!

I pulled my van into the stillness of my garage as the darkness surrendered to the ceiling light's illumination. Turning off the engine, I laid my head against the steering wheel. *Lord*, I prayed, my spirit calming, *I transfer all my faith from myself to You.* In my mind's eye, I could see Jesus' loving face as I handed Him back the limp body of my daughter. *Lord, she is Yours*, I prayed. *I am going to trust You with her future. My faith in You no longer depends upon her healing, for, as in the words of Job in Job 13:15,*

"Though he slay me, yet will I trust in him" (KJV).

Like release won from the Chinese finger puzzle, I no longer struggle against myself but push toward God. I am free indeed.

The Visitor in the Elevator

I'd never been homeless until Laura lay in a Texas ICU hospital bed, hooked to monitors and life-support equipment. My Colorado home was two thousand miles away, and my mom was still a patient in the hospital across town. Although my husband and my father pleaded with me to spend my nights in the guest bedroom of my parents' home, I refused. Instead, I spent my time perched on a stool, clutching Laura's hand, so afraid she would slip away if I let go.

But the nuns who ran the hospital were compassionate and offered to let me sleep in one of the empty rooms on the floor that was being remodeled. I accepted, glad I would be only seconds from my daughter's side.

By day, the workers remodeled the floor of my hospital home while I sat in ICU with Laura. But every night, around midnight, I would ride the elevator down to the deserted floor, walk down the dimly lighted hall, and step inside my room before shutting the door and twisting its flimsy lock. Then I'd check the shower stall to be sure I was alone before pushing several pieces of heavy furniture against the door to the hall.

Even if someone tries to break in, my security measures will give me time to use my phone to call for help, I reasoned.

One night, after a fruitless day of waiting for Laura to stir, I rode the elevator down to my floor. After I walked down the hall to my room, I found the door locked—and I did not have a key. That meant I had to walk back to the empty nurses' station situated directly in front of the elevator doors and call security. "We'll be up to unlock your door in just a few minutes," someone promised.

I sat in the empty station, ready to greet the officer as soon as the polished elevator doors opened.

As I waited, a still, quiet voice spoke to my spirit. "Get up, walk across the hall, and stand by the wall," it seemed to say.

I shook my head sleepily. *What a silly idea. From that vantage point, I won't be able to see inside the elevator when the security officer arrives!* I thought, not wanting to budge from the comfort of my padded chair.

Again, I heard the voice. This time, it spoke more forcibly. "Get up, walk across the hall, and stand by the wall."

Slowly I rose and walked out from behind the granite-topped desk. As I stepped in front of the elevator door, its down-arrow glowed red, and the doors began to slide open.

At last, I thought, *someone from security has come to let me into my room.*

Still, I continued my slow walk to the wall. As I did, the elevator doors slid in pace with my quiet, tennis-shoed steps.

I looked back, trying to see who was inside, but to no avail. *Well, where is the officer? I can hear him breathing. Why doesn't he come out?*

When I reached the wall, I stopped and turned around. The elevator doors were now wide open, and a yellow light spilled onto the polished floor of the darkened foyer. Still, I couldn't see who was inside the metal cavity.

I started to walk back the way I had come, still trying to crane my neck for a peek inside the opened doors. As I walked forward, the doors of the elevator began to slide shut, in perfect tempo with my pace.

Before I caught a glimpse of my visitor, the doors sealed with a clang. Bewildered, I stood in front of the closed doors and stared at my dim reflection. *Why had I acted so strangely? If I had stayed seated at the nurses' station, I could have greeted the security officer when the elevator doors opened, and he'd be opening the door to my room right now.*

Although, I realized, it was strange that he didn't step out. *But too late now. He's gone.*

I returned to my seat at the nurses' desk and called security again. "Someone will be there shortly," the man said.

Cradling my head with my arms, I rested it on the desk.

Some time later, I was startled by the scurry of footsteps. I blinked sleepily as two nurses rounded the corner. They stared in surprise.

"What are you doing here?" a male nurse asked gruffly.

"I'm waiting for a security guard to let me into my room."

"You'd better come with us!" the female nurse responded. "There is a stalker in the hospital tonight. He's attacked several women. It is not safe for you to be alone."

I felt the color drain from my face; suddenly, it all made sense. The man in the elevator had not been the security guard. I had almost come face to face with a potential rapist. If I hadn't obeyed the still, quiet voice, I might have been attacked!

Meekly, I followed the nurses to their station, several floors above mine, and slept fitfully on their waiting-room couch.

Psalm 119:60 says,

"I will hasten and not delay to obey your commands."

This is good advice. How glad I was I had listened to my Master's voice and had obeyed His directives. I am certain His call saved me from the nightmare of an assault. How grateful I am He was there to counsel me to safety.

Medicated Bandages

14

God's Word can be like medicine. Proverbs 4:20-22 says,

*"Listen closely to my words. Do not let them
out of your sight, keep them within your heart;
for they are life to those who find them
and health to a man's whole body."*

But medicine, I've noticed, is often unpleasant to take.
At least my young son thinks so. Take the day Jimmy got a
scratch on his hand.

Being a smart four-year-old, he knew that I kept the bandages in Laura's room. He stood in the doorway. "Nurse," he lisped, "I need a bandage. I got an owie on my hand."

As Laura's nurse, Carol, helped him get a bandage out of the drawer, she said, "Let me put a little medicine on your cut for you."

"OK," Jimmy agreed. "But don't put the medicine under the bandage—put it on top of the bandage."

"But the medicine won't help your cut if I put it on the bandage," Carol said, trying to hide a smile.

Jimmy batted his blond lashes. "But if you put the medicine on my cut, it will sting."

"Well, I think that's the point. The medicine will sting, but it will kill the germs too."

How valid Jimmy's concerns were. Medicine does sting our cuts. Yet, as Carol pointed out, it kills germs and promotes healing.

This is also true with God's Word. When I apply it directly to my situations, it often stings. But as God's Word stings me, it kills the germs of hate and envy. Also, the power of God's Word promotes healing.

How healthful it is to take a dose of God's Word every day. It may take extra effort, but even when it stings, it purifies as it speaks to my heart.

The Perfect Baby?

When I became pregnant again, my fears grew along with my girth. *How am I ever going to make this work? Maybe Paul and I shouldn't have had a second child while Laura still needs so much care.*

Hugging my tummy, I cried out to God, asking that He bring us a baby that would "fit" into our household.

Laura had been the perfect baby, and I wanted another baby just like her—sweet natured, full of smiles, and easy to care for. My worst fears were that I would have a baby with the infamous Evans' temperament—like my brother, Jimmy.

I could still remember when my green-eyed brother hit

two. It was a terrible time indeed. The fits he could throw included flying chairs, screaming, and kicking tantrums.

What if my unborn baby turned out to be like him? With all the added turmoil of my life, this possibility frightened me. So I'd pat my tummy, kiss Laura, and continue to pray, *O Lord, please let this baby fit in!*

I should have known better, but when the ultrasound showed our baby to be a boy, Paul and I decided we would name him James Paul—Jimmy, for short. And when the moment came for me to hold my eight-pound, four-ounce baby in my arms for the first time, my heart sank. I knew what we were in for.

Jimmy, who had squeezed into this life with his umbilical cord wrapped around his neck, still howled in anger two hours after his birth. And now I held a screaming, clenched-fist, red-faced infant. As I held my wailing son, I prayed, *Lord, how will I ever manage this strong-willed child?*

But as I look back, how thankful I am that now-seven-year-old Jimmy demanded my attention as much as he did. Although difficult at times, he ended up fitting in perfectly. God knew what He was doing, after all. For as it says in Romans 8:28,

> *"We know that in all things God works*
> *for the good of those who love him,*
> *who have been called according to his purpose."*

As I watch my son's sensitive spirit blossom and see how much love he and Laura share with one another, I recognize the wisdom God demonstrated when He placed Jimmy into our family. How proud I am Jimmy continues to "fit" so perfectly into our home.

Flood Assurance 16

Crisis can call anytime, slicing through the stillness of night with bad news.

Not long ago, my phone rang. "Your dad and I can't believe it," my mom said, sounding shell-shocked. "We never thought the floodwaters would reach our house. But they did. I've just been evacuated in a large dump truck."

When the floodwaters began creeping under the door of my parents' beautiful new home in Bevil Oaks, outside of Beaumont, Texas, all she had time to pack was one suitcase of clothes.

"All the other women in the dump truck were weeping," Mom said. "But not me. I was glad to be escaping with my life. That's the most important thing."

"Where's Dad?"

"He's still at the house, trying to put a few things in the attic."

I caught my breath. How high were those floodwaters, anyway? Dad had fallen down the attic steps once before. What if he slipped and landed face down in the water while he was alone?

I was relieved when he finally phoned.

"I was very careful," he assured me. "The water was ankle deep, and I had to use my electric power saw to cut wood so I could put our furniture on blocks!"

What! I really was grateful he was now on higher ground.

Dad continued, "When the water first started to rise, I let the dog into the house. Bo looked up at your mother, expecting her usual demand for him to get out, but this time, Verna only shrugged and said, 'Bo, you might as well come in.'

"Later, when Bo and I got into the dump truck," Dad continued, "many of the people were crying. Bo didn't know what to do. So he sat down on the muddy floor and tried to cheer us up with an occasional wag of his tail. But each time his tail thumped, he sloshed mud on our legs.

"Finally, I scolded him. But one of the women said, 'Never mind him. Why, that's nothing.' "

She was right. Things were suddenly in perspective. With all the loss of the day, having a wet Australian sheep dog running through your new house or splashing mud on your legs was nothing.

But through the devastation of that east Texas flood, there

was good news. All the neighbors survived the ordeal, and many went back to clean their homes and lay new carpet.

This reminds me of what Jesus taught in Matthew 7:24, 25:

"Everyone who hears these words of mine and puts them into practice is like a wise man who built his house on the rock. The rain came down, the streams rose, and the winds blew and beat against that house; yet it did not fall, because it had its foundation on the rock."

As for me, when I am founded on God's Word, I'm equipped to face sudden crisis. The Bible is the best foundation I'll ever find for building a life.

17

The Happies

When Jimmy was small, we chose not to allow him to go trick-or-treating because I wanted to avoid celebrating Halloween. But in an attempt to show love to our neighbors, Jimmy helped me hand out candy to the trick-or-treaters who came to our door. Jimmy was young enough that he had not figured out he was the only child without a costume or a bag of candy.

One day in late October when Jimmy was three, a friendly grocery-store clerk asked my young son, "So, what are you going to be for Halloween?"

I held my breath, wondering how little Jimmy would answer. I laughed as he gleefully squealed, "Happy!"

Later, when I thought about Jimmy's answer, it made me wonder if I'd always recognized appropriate times to be happy. Many blessings come my way, but at times I'm too busy or too preoccupied to notice or acknowledge them.

Sometimes, I'm simply too embarrassed to count them. Recently, Jimmy and I ran some errands downtown. Because Jimmy wasn't feeling well, I let him take his red-and-yellow tape recorder into the print-shop to help him entertain himself while I ran off some copies. Standing next to the purring copy machine, I hadn't realized how loud Jimmy's Sesame Street sing-along tape sounded to the print shop patrons. Suddenly, Jimmy turned the volume of the peppy music even higher and jumped up from the floor. "Let's dance!" he shouted.

My eyes wide, I watched Jimmy gyrate in the middle of the print-shop floor, beckoning me to join his fun.

"Mommy's busy right now," I said, embarrassed. I turned my head to sneak a peak at the print-shop staff. Were they watching the show? My mouth fell open. All the workers, owner included, had stopped working and were doing the twist to Jimmy's Sesame Street music!

I laughed at all the happiness around me. This time, I couldn't ignore everyone's glee.

Proverbs 16:20 says,

"Whoever trusts in the Lord, happy is he" (NKJV).

Like trusting in God, happiness is something we choose. It springs out of us when we acknowledge our blessings.

Will you join me?

Faith Never Shrinks in Hot Water

The pain in Sheila's blue eyes caught me off guard. "I want to talk to you in private," she said. "I think you may be the only person who can understand what I'm going through."

"Of course," I said as we picked up our lunch sacks and slipped out of the conference we were attending. My new friend and I set up an impromptu picnic in an empty classroom.

"What's on your mind, Sheila?" I asked, pulling my sandwich from my bag.

Sheila wiped her eyes with her napkin and stared into her lap. "I have a teenage daughter who is mentally ill. And I've done everything I can to help her, but she's not getting better. Instead, she's getting worse—more violent. I've prayed and prayed, but I feel like my prayers are hitting the ceiling. I still consider myself a Christian, even though it seems as if God is for everyone else, but He's not for me."

I touched my friend's hand, and she looked up. "I've been there, Sheila. When Laura spent ten months in a coma, I, too, felt cut off from God."

"I knew you must have," Sheila confided.

"What I've learned is that you can't go by appearances."

Sheila unwrapped her sandwich and asked, "What do you mean?"

"When Laura was in a coma, it seemed as if God was nowhere around. But He was there. On the surface, the waves were stormy, but it was in the cool, peaceful depths where God was working—the depths where I could not see.

"I thought that God had deaf ears and that Laura was going to stay in her coma forever. But God was awakening her, even when I did not realize He was at work."

Sheila complained, "But God does not seem to be at work in our situation. Amy's tantrums are getting more violent. Plus, the kids at school call her 'Retard.' Do you know what that does to her self-esteem? It's trashed!

"On top of that, Amy's medication is having bad side effects. She's more moody than ever. And because Christians often have a hard time understanding and dealing with mental illness, we are not getting a lot of support. Even Amy's teacher thinks my daughter's problems are my fault. Mrs. Smith says if my faith were stronger, God would heal Amy!"

"That is a lot for you to be carrying around. Let's talk first about the teacher's comment—if her assessment about your faith is correct, then let me ask, Where is her faith? Her reasoning is illogical. If she believes God will heal Amy if someone's faith is strong enough, then why isn't her faith strong enough?" I countered.

"Besides, that is not how God works. We can't hold a gun to God and demand that He do what we say because we claim we have enough faith. Instead, we have to trust Him— to believe He is all-powerful, powerful enough to heal Amy or powerful enough to help us through our struggles. This is what true faith is all about."

Sheila smiled a tiny smile. "Then I do have faith!"

I nodded. "If you believe in God's power, you have a faith that will never shrink in hot water. Just don't accept false guilt, Sheila. You don't need it."

"If only you knew how hard I've tried to help my daughter. We're in biblical counseling. I've prayed until I was exhausted; I've wept until my tears were spent. But nothing seems to work. It seems God just doesn't care."

"God does care! And He is with you. It's just that He's moving in ways you don't recognize or understand."

"What do you mean?"

"Is Amy getting any positive support?" I asked.

Sheila's eyes lighted up. "Yes, a friend at church has taken a special interest in her and takes her horseback riding every weekend! It's been really neat."

"That's wonderful! I'd say God is behind that! What about Amy herself?" I asked. "Has God given her any special gifts?"

Sheila nodded. "Her tender heart! She loves children and

always protects them from the schoolyard bullies!"

"That's fabulous! That's God again!"

"Then why do I feel so cut off from Him?" Sheila asked.

"You feel cut off because you are in a season of grief. This season will not last forever. Besides, life is full of seasons. Ecclesiastes 3:1 says: 'To everything there is a season, a time for every purpose under heaven' (NKJV).

"Someday," I told Sheila, "like Job in the Old Testament, you will move beyond your season of grief, and you will know that in the midst of your former sorrow, you were never alone. One of my favorite verses is Psalm 126:6:

'He who continually goes forth weeping,
bearing seed for sowing, shall doubtless come again
with rejoicing, bringing his sheaves with him' (NKJV).

"Even when you cannot hear God's voice or feel His presence, His love for you does not change. He has not forgotten you as you sow your tears of sorrow, and He is moving in ways you have yet to imagine. Your seeds of love and faith are taking root for the harvest to come."

Getting Carried Away

Life is full of wearing experiences, from forging a spiritual journey to shopping with toddlers. As a brave mother, I often dragged my young son to places other parents and tots never ventured without strollers equipped with locking seat belts.

But by the time Jimmy was three, strollers were no longer an option, for his little fingers could unlock seat-belt buckles with ease. Still, Jimmy and I often braved the world of shopping, not until one of us dropped, but until one of us lost our cool.

On one long trip to the mall, I had boldly walked little Jimmy to the food court to meet his dad for a Chinese dinner. For dessert, Paul and I indulged in a little window shopping, with Jimmy in tow. Surprisingly, Jimmy did well, not even "losing his control" when we passed his favorite ice-cream shop.

At eight-thirty, Paul and I decided to head for home. Paul left us to walk to his truck, parked near the food-court entrance, while Jimmy and I began the long journey through the mall to our van.

As we passed through Sears, Jimmy suddenly flopped to the tile floor. "I'm tired," he said, grabbing my right snow boot in a finger-locking grasp. "Could you drag me for a while?"

I tried to pull free of Jimmy's grip as a couple of sales-clerks giggled. "Honey, we're almost to the van," I whispered, looking down at the top of his white-blond head. "Why don't you walk?"

Jimmy clung to my black boot. "I'm too tired. Drag me, Mom. Please?"

I leaned over him. "I don't think I can drag you, but I can carry you. Would that be OK?"

Jimmy looked up and nodded, so I scooped him into my arms. His eyelids closed as he relaxed into a sleeping lump of dead weight.

As I carried my sleeping child, I thought how his pleading compared with my own spiritual journey. Instead of asking God to carry me when I'm tired, I often throw myself at His feet. "Drag me," I cry.

It's easy to forget that I'm one of God's children. He's a good Father and doesn't want to rake me through the muck. He longs to scoop me into His arms and carry me. And

when I let Him, I can safely rest.
   Deuteronomy 33:27 says,

> *"The eternal God is your refuge,*
> *and underneath are the everlasting arms."*

What a beautiful image of God, my refuge. Because He holds me, my worries fall away. I can always rest assured in Him, even when I am shopping with an exhausted toddler.

Starry Motivators

Sometimes my kids and I need a big dose of motivation. For example, when Jimmy was four, we had major battles each time I asked him to eat his breakfast, brush his teeth, or go to bed. I tried everything—coaxing, pleading, punishing, and timeouts. Nothing worked. I was sure I was failing the counsel of Proverbs 22:6 to

"train a child in the way he should go."

Then one afternoon, while shopping in a department store, we passed a six-dollar gumball machine. "Oh, Mom," Jimmy said, his eyes wide, "I really need that."

Instead of my usual No, I stopped to remember an early-morning prayer. *Lord*, I had prayed, *give me an idea that will help me motivate Jimmy to good behavior!*

And there it was in front of me, an orb of blue plastic, for a mere $5.99—a true bargain.

I looked down at my young son. "Do you *really* want this gumball machine?" I asked.

Jimmy nodded earnestly.

"All right," I said. "But you're going to have to earn it."

"How, Mommy?" he asked.

I wheeled our cart over to the office supplies and picked up a fluorescent yellow posterboard, marker, and stick-on stars.

"With a star chart!" I said.

Suddenly, there were no more tears when I announced it was bedtime. Instead, it became a game. "Can you put your pajamas on before the kitchen timer buzzes? If you can, you will earn a star!"

Now I had the ultimate punishment: "If you don't put your toys away in the next five minutes, I'm taking a star off your chart!"

But as I bragged about Jimmy's improving obedience to Laura's nurses, I began to notice that Laura would pucker her lips into a pout. Could it be Laura wanted a star chart too? I wondered.

When I told Laura she could have her own chart, her face broke into a smile the size of Colorado. Eagerly, she improved her mealtimes with the nurses. They'd say, "Laura, if you don't bite the spoon when I feed you lunch, you'll get a star!"

When Laura earned her first seventy-five stars, she was thrilled to get a new blouse.

I can't believe how well the star charts have motivated my children. It makes me realize how much I need to find motivations for my personal and spiritual goals. Maybe I'm too old to have a motivational star chart. But I can take time to reflect on how far I've grown, managed my temper, or gotten along with my family.

I still have my shortcomings, but I'm making progress. And I'm looking forward to the day when I can lay a star-studded crown at Jesus' throne.

Party Balloons

When four-year-old Jimmy and I were driving through our neighborhood, he happened to see a red helium balloon escape into the clouds.

"Look, Mom! That balloon is going to heaven so Jesus can have a party!"

As I thought about Jimmy's idea of sending God a party balloon, I wondered whether my prayers could be a colorful balloon bouquet to God as well.

Although my feet are tethered to the pain of this earth, because I know Christ, there is always a reason to send God a bundle of praise and thanksgiving.

When Laura graduated from kindergarten, we decided to

commemorate the event with a tea party for her and her friends. Soon, seven little girls, dressed in their mothers' clothes and high heels, rang our doorbell. We celebrated the afternoon with cake, lemonade, games, and giggles.

Unfortunately, I ran out of activities before I ran out of time. So I told the girls they could go into Laura's room and look at her medical equipment.

A few minutes later, I had seven giggly girls on Laura's wheelchair lift. As I stood with them, pressing the down-button, an abandoned gallon of spoiled milk, perched on the shelf high above our heads, exploded. The girls screamed as spoiled milk rained down on us.

At that same moment, the lift threw a breaker and halted in midair.

"What happened?" one of the girls cried, wringing out her feather boa.

"Have you ever heard of a milk bath?" I asked.

"Pew! It stinks!" another girl wailed, pouring milk off her straw hat.

"Yes," I said, "but you know what they say, 'Never cry over spilt milk.' "

I was amazed at what happened next. Instead of tears and wails of anguish, the girls burst into giggles. Our spilled milk hadn't soured the party but turned it into a milkshake.

Later, as I thought about it, I was thankful the explosion of milk hadn't popped my balloon of praise. After all, 1 Thessalonians 5:16-18 says,

"Be joyful always; pray continually;
give thanks in all circumstances,
for this is God's will for you in Christ Jesus."

Despite the spoiled-milk catastrophe, there were many things to be thankful for. Even though Laura had been severely disabled in a car accident, she had graduated from kindergarten, and she had celebrated the event with her friends. This was no time for burst bubbles; this was a time to send a balloon of praise and thankfulness to heaven and to invite God to celebrate our joy.

Lost Legs

Sometimes it's hard to walk where we are supposed to. Jimmy and I both learned this lesson when he was four. We were just snuggling down to watch a video when the doorbell rang.

"Hi!" Andrew, our tall, lanky eleven-year-old neighbor, greeted me. "I was wondering if I could walk Jackson around the block?"

"Sure," I said, gathering up our new puppy and his leash. Jimmy asked, "May I go, Mom? Please?"

"No. Not this time. Besides, you haven't been able to find your other tennis shoe all afternoon."

Snuggling back onto the couch, I continued to watch the

video. A few minutes later, I heard the sound that every parent of small children fears: silence!

I ran to Jimmy's room to check on him. He wasn't there. As I began to call him, panic edged my voice. I rushed into Laura's room to look. He wasn't there either. Laura's nurse asked, "Where do you think he is?"

"I bet he found his lost shoe and slipped out of the house to find Andrew! Only thing is, he doesn't know how to cross the street by himself!"

Laura began to cry in fright.

"I'll find him," I called as I grabbed my keys and ran to the gray van. I backed out of the driveway carefully, just in case he was darting about the front yard. When I hit the street, I gunned it. Before I'd traveled half a block, I spotted Andrew and a leashed ball of fluff heading in my direction.

"Have you seen Jimmy?" I screamed.

Andrew froze. "He's missing?"

"I think he went to look for you," I shouted as I hit the gas pedal.

A twisting quarter-mile away, I spotted my young son, with his hands in his pockets, shuffling along a golden-leaf-covered sidewalk. Honking my horn like a maniac, I squealed the brakes of the van.

He smiled and waved, glad to see me.

What happened next probably looked like a kidnapping. I swung open the van door and leapt to the sidewalk, where I grabbed Jimmy into my arms. "Where do you think you are going?" I shouted in hysteria. "I told you, you couldn't go for a walk!" I carried him to the van and sped away.

Between his sobs, Jimmy said, "My legs didn't know I couldn't go."

When we got home, I took five stars off his motivational chart. "You are too young to walk by yourself," I explained. "Taking off these stars will help your legs remember that they're not to go for walks without asking first."

That night, as I lay my head upon my pillow, I thought about what King David had said in Psalm 48:14:

*"This God is our God for ever and ever;
he will be our guide even to the end."*

I stopped to pray. *Lead me, Lord. Don't let my legs take a mind of their own. Help me to walk with You.*

Bad Puppy

We have an adorable white ball of fluff named Jackson. At least he seems adorable, but as I so often remind him, he's a real dog.

I rather doubt that Jackson realizes he is an animal. True, he loves to sort through the trash and eat dirty tissues, but he also delights in hamburger and pancake snatching—even if it means a scolding and a timeout in his dog run. Jackson simply licks his chops and sniffs the air for more.

Recently, Paul, Jimmy, and I were out of town. Laura, the nurses, and Jackson were at home, minding the fort. Pam, Laura's speech therapist and a great admirer of Jackson, thought it would be a wonderful idea to bring our dog home to play with her son for the weekend. Had I been there, I would have been able to warn her as to what she was getting herself into. But, alas, Pam decided to be kind to my pet in my absence.

Once in her home, our long-legged Jackson began to belie his sweet-puppy appearance. At the first opportunity, he bolted out Pam's front door and raced down the street.

For some reason, the moment this small, poodlelike dog is free from the confines of fence and house, he points his nose in any direction and follows it as fast as his legs allow.

It was in this manner that he led the entire Hyink family on a two-hour chase of hide-and-seek before capture.

After the chase, Pam decided to confine Jackson to her kitchen for the rest of the weekend. But she hadn't counted on a small hole in her screen door and Jackson's fondness for chasing cats.

When Jackson returned from his unleashed run, he made a beeline for Pam's cat. The cat hissed and bristled her fur before Pam unlatched the screen door and let her onto the back porch. As the screen door slammed shut, Jackson threw his body at a small tear in the screen and broke through!

The startled cat leapt off the porch and onto the adjoining roof of Pam's garage. Jackson followed in a flash.

The cat ran up the slanted roof and perched on its uppermost pinnacle. Jackson bounded toward her, and the feline leapt gracefully to the grassy earth. Undaunted, Jackson flung himself after her. But his flight ended with a thud.

Jackson stood on trembling legs and shook his head while Pam rushed to recapture him. With Jackson tucked under one arm, Pam grabbed her car keys and rushed him to her vet.

One vet bill, a broken screen door, and a ruined after-noon later, Jackson, no worse for his adventure, was on his way back to our house.

Pam now laughs when she recalls the weekend. She says, "I'm just relieved I didn't have to tell your kids I lost their dog!" And she adds, "It wasn't all bad; I got to meet several of my neighbors who joined us in the chase."

Although Jackson has had far more than his share of memorable escapades, when he curls in my lap to take a nap, I almost believe he's really as sweet as he looks. As it says in Ecclesiastes 9:4,

"For him who is joined to all the living there is hope, for a living dog is better than a dead lion" (NKJV).

And as long as Jackson's living, I can always hope he will learn to be more prudent.

Knifed in the Eye

I'm learning to hear God's voice, one day at a time. One of my early experiences in learning to listen came the day I decided to cook a frozen mini-pizza for lunch.

"Can I help?" Jimmy asked.

"You can get out the cookie sheet and put the pizza on top," I replied.

But when I turned my back to fill our glasses with ice, Jimmy reached for a sharp knive and tried to poke a hole in the cellophane wrap that covered the pizza. As he did, the point of the knife skated across the plastic surface and flew up and into his eye.

The next moment, Jimmy screamed, and the knife clattered across the linoleum.

I grabbed Jimmy as his eyes closed and he fell limp into my arms. Still cradling Jimmy, I ran to the phone and called our eye doctor. "It's an emergency!" I said. "My three-year-old has poked a knife in his eye! He seems to be unconscious!"

"Bring him right in," the receptionist said.

I rushed him to the van. *Why is he so limp?* I wondered. *Could the point of the knife have penetrated through his eye and into his brain?* Fortunately, heavy traffic slowed my impulse to drive like a maniac to the doctor's office.

I should pray! Suddenly I thought of Jesus' words in John 10:27,

> *"My sheep hear My voice, and I know them, and they follow Me" (NKJV).*

With new perception, I prayed, *Lord, did You see what happened? Will Jimmy lose his eye? Did the knife puncture his brain?* I listened intently. A still, small voice spoke to my heart. "Jimmy will be OK."

Is that You, Lord? I wondered as I pulled into the doctor's office parking lot. My young son was still unconscious, yet I felt a peace as I rushed him inside.

"I can't believe you are so calm," the receptionist commented. After what seemed like hours, the doctor called us in to see him, and we gently shook Jimmy to arouse him.

After carefully examining Jimmy's eye with fluorescent dye, the doctor finally announced, "He's got a tiny nick on the edge of his lower eyelid. But the eye itself is not damaged."

"Why did he go limp?" I asked.

"He fainted," the doctor replied. "Nicks on the eyelid really hurt."

When Jimmy and I left the doctor's office, I felt grateful. Not only was Jimmy OK, but I knew beyond a shadow of a doubt that the Holy Spirit had really spoken to me. All it took was my willingness to ask and to listen for His voice.

Maybe I should listen more often.

The Best Gift

What's the most important gift a person can give? My daughter gives it often, even though she has to sit in a wheel-chair and does not have the ability to speak.

Sometimes I get tired of dealing with people who inquire about her. Usually our conversation starts with the casual question "Do you have any children?"

I try to avoid saying I have a child who has a disability because the person asking the question is usually not ready to get emotionally involved with my problems.

But their original "Do you have kids?" question is usually followed by "What school does your daughter go to?"

Unfortunately, this probe seems to open the door to conversational disaster.

"Laura goes to two schools," I explain, "one for kids with special needs and one for typical kids."

"Special needs?" I'm asked. "Is your daughter all right?"

Inwardly, I grimace. I've been down this road of explanation before, and I know what is about to happen. "She's a happy little girl," I say. "But she has a disability."

"What's wrong?"

"She was in a car accident when she was eighteen months old," I explain.

Desperate to make Laura's situation all right, they ask, "But she's OK now, right?"

To me, this is a difficult question. Of course, I think she's OK. I know she's *only* a person with a disability. I also know my interviewers won't understand that. So I say, "Well, Laura's in a wheelchair."

More uncomfortable than ever, they ask, "But she can talk and stuff, right?"

I sigh. There's no way out of this one. "No, but she can communicate with tongue signals."

By this time, my interviewer is at a loss for words. So I try to help out. "But you know, Laura's a happy little girl who really enjoys her life."

The person nods mutely and steps back as if ready to make a run for it.

I step closer. "She really is a happy child. And she has lots of friends."

"Oh," my interviewer responds in a whisper. "She's lucky she has you for a mother."

I force a smile and say, "As far as I'm concerned, I'm just

a mother who is lucky to have such a sweet kid for a daughter!"

My questioner excuses himself or herself, I'm left feeling unsettled. If only I could explain the validity of Laura's life in a way the casual conversationalist could understand. Unfortunately, our society is not taught to recognize the viability of a life that can offer nothing to the world except love. First Corinthians 13:1, 2 says:

"Though I speak with the tongues of men
and of angels, but have not love, I have become as
sounding brass or a clanging cymbal.
And though I have the gift of prophecy,
and understand all mysteries and all knowledge,
and though I have all faith, so that I could remove
mountains, but have not love, I am nothing" (NKJV).

I think the gift of love Laura so freely gives is worth more than any other gift that even an abled-bodied person can offer. I have a child who not only receives love but radiates love to all those around her. I am a fortunate mother indeed.

Hiding From God

"Mom," five-year-old Jimmy asked, "where can I hide from God?"

I smiled at him. "Honey, God can see you wherever you are."

"Could He see me if I hid behind the couch?" he asked, slipping behind it.

"Of course," I answered.

Jimmy peeked over the back cushion. "What if I hid in an airplane in the sky?"

"God would see you there too," I answered.

"What if I hid under the sea with the fish?" Jimmy asked, climbing over the back of the couch and sliding onto the decorative pillows. "I bet He couldn't find me there!"

I rubbed the top of Jimmy's head. "God could see you there too. In fact, there is no place you can go where you can hide from God."

Jimmy's face fell. "You mean He can see me even when I'm doing something I shouldn't?"

I raised my brows. "Well, yes. Were you planning to do something you shouldn't?"

Jimmy sagged against a pillow. "Never mind," he said evasively. "I guess I'll be good today."

Maybe Jimmy came to the right conclusion. After all, Psalm 139:1 says,

*"O Lord, You have searched me
and known me" (NKJV).*

It is scary to realize God is always watching me—even when I loose my cool or exceed the speed limit. But what's even more sobering is to know He hears all my thoughts!

But if I were to stay aware of God's presence, then perhaps I would be more careful about guarding my heart and tongue.

I like what my friend Pam does. As she gets into her van to make home visits to disabled and speech-delayed children throughout Boulder County, she clears off the seat next to her. "I reserve this seat for Jesus," she says. In this way, Pam reminds herself of His presence throughout her day.

What a great idea! When I'm tempted to think or say

something I shouldn't, I might be wise to see who's sitting on the throne of my heart. If I did, I'd be sure to flop onto the couch next to little Jimmy and say, "Never mind! I'll be good too."

27

Confessions of a Fibber

Have you ever told a whopper? Has your victim ever believed you? Have you ever wondered how you were able to get away with it? I'm sorry to say that I have.

I'll always remember the time our tri-level house was on the market. A potential buyer, touring our home, peeked into Laura's mini-ICU bedroom.

"What's wrong with your daughter?" she demanded, hands on her hips, staring at my still-comatose child.

I flinched. *Oh no, not that conversation!* I mentally sighed. *I'm just too tired to deal with upsetting this stranger today.*

Before I knew it, a lie escaped my lips. "Nothing is wrong with her," I cooed to my guest. I folded my arms.

"Laura's just taking a nap!"

The woman looked delighted. "Oh!" she said, her steps lighter as she continued her tour.

I couldn't believe it! By all appearances, that woman seemed to have actually believed me. Why? I think because she wanted to! And even though I felt ashamed of telling a lie, I learned something. People will believe what they want to believe.

People will believe what they want about God, as well. Sure, there are many false teachings in the world, but as Paul says in Romans 1:20,

"Since the creation of the world His invisible attributes are clearly seen, being understood by the things that are made, even His eternal power and Godhead, so that they are without excuse."

I guess it's somewhat like my deceived guest. The evidence of an ill or injured child was clearly visible. Just by looking around, this woman could see a child sleeping in a special bed, a wheelchair, a nurse sitting in a rocking chair, life-support equipment, and feeding bags hanging from poles. But she chose to believe my lie.

Now, mind you, I'm not criticizing this woman. I was the one who led her into the falsehood, but isn't it interesting that I could get away with it?

Like this woman who believed my lie, many of us believe lies about God. Think of all the evidence we have seen, and yet many of us ignore the evidence and believe in unproven modern "theory tales."

But when I look around, I can see God's handiwork everywhere. I see it when I take a moonlit stroll into my backyard and look up at the stars. I see it when I watch an ant crawling up a blade of grass. And when I look into the eyes of a newborn baby, I see God's miraculous signature.

The evidence speaks volumes. Forget what you may have been told, and see the truth for yourself. God's truths are everywhere you look.

28
Discovering Common Ground

Even though my now-nine-year-old daughter, Laura, is severely disabled and can communicate only through tongue signals, she is like other girls her age in many ways—her mother has the power to embarrass her terribly! The first time I discovered this was when she was in preschool.

Laura's teacher thought it would be a good idea for me to come with Laura and explain her disabilities to the other kids. As I finished explaining Laura's limitations, wheel-chair, and life-support system, my eyes met hers, and I knew—Laura was mortified. I thought she'd never forgive me.

A few years later, Laura's second-grade teacher suggested that

I come into the classroom to talk to Laura's classmates about my daughter. I was concerned, and so was Laura. What could I say to the kids that wouldn't embarrass my sensitive child?

The morning came, and Laura frowned as I walked into her classroom. "Laura," I asked, "would you like to come to the front of the room with me as I talk to your friends?"

Laura sat in her purple wheelchair and made a pointed No sign with her tongue and shut her eyes. I hesitated. This was going to be tougher than I had thought.

"I'm Laura's mom," I started out, addressing the other children. "And I want to tell you something about Laura."

Laura stuck out her lower lip. "I just want all of you to know how much Laura's dad, brother, and I love her."

Her tightly shut eyelids fluttered.

"I want you to know how glad we are Laura is our little girl."

A slight smile spread across Laura's pretty face, and she peeked out of one eye.

A little boy raised his hand and asked hesitantly, "How come Laura is in a wheelchair?"

Laura squeezed her eyes shut again. "You know, Laura doesn't like for me to talk about that. But let me say, Laura was hurt in a car accident. How many of you have ever been hurt and had to go to the hospital?"

Twenty children raised their hands, all eager to share their stories. "Wow," I said with surprise, "that's almost everyone."

I noticed Laura peeking again.

"Then most of you can understand what Laura went through," I continued.

A little girl, dressed in pink pants and matching teddy-bear-print T-shirt, raised her hand. "I just want you to know we all love Laura very much." The other children nodded their agreement.

Eyes wide open, Laura grinned from ear to ear.

By the end of my time with the children, Laura was still smiling and greatly relieved that her mom had not embarrassed her.

Isn't it funny? Until that day, Laura did not know how many ways she was like her friends. And I learned how much the other children identified with and loved her. What an exciting surprise! It only proves that Jesus' challenge in John 13:34 to

"love one another"

is more than just a nice thought. For, as Jesus knows, a little love can bridge the impossible.

Slaying Dragons
29

Five-year-old Jimmy had been spending the evening with his sister. After whispering secrets into her ear, he gave her a big kiss on the cheek, then moved to the desk to draw her a few pictures.

His recurring theme seemed to be great fire-breathing dragons scorching spiders. When he was through, he looked up at Nurse Sharon. "I'm going to leave these in here for Laura tonight," he said.

"That would be nice," Sharon said.

Jimmy's face clouded as he sifted through his winged-dragon drawings. "I just hope these pictures stay on the paper and don't turn real before morning."

I laughed when Sharon repeated the story to me. "You know," I commented, "maybe that kid's onto something. These dragon drawings are a lot like our worries."

"Why do you say that?" Sharon asked with a mischievous grin.

"How often do we paint worries in our minds, then hope they don't become real?"

Sharon laughed. "Too often, I guess."

But, I wondered later, *what should we do with our imagined dragons? How can we slay what isn't real?* As I have thought about this dilemma, I have come to realize I'm not in control of my life in the first place. The best thing I can do is to give the control I never had to God. When I do, I'm no longer afraid of the dragons I paint in my worries. Even if they do come to life, I have a God whom I can trust to see me through. Psalm 95:7 says,

"He is our God and we are the people of his pasture, the flock under his care."

What a relief it is to rely on Him, instead of myself, to slay my dragons. After all, His care is really the safest place to be.

Scratching Where It Itches

A winter-pale Jimmy played in the water sprinkler one warm spring day. I hadn't realized the afternoon sun was already capable of blushing his white shoulders with a deep-red burn—that is, until it was too late. Later, I rubbed cool lotion onto Jimmy's burning skin.

"Jimmy, maybe this will help your burn feel better!"

But even this soothing lotion did not prevent Jimmy's back from peeling.

A couple of days later, a shirtless Jimmy backed up to me. "Mom," he said, looking over his shoulder, "Please scratch my back."

I tickled the scaly white patches of dead skin on Jimmy's

back with my fingernails. As I did, Jimmy's blue eyes peeked from beneath his fringe of cotton hair. "No, Mom," he said, exasperated. "Not there. Scratch where it itches!"

I had to laugh. "Jimmy, you are going to have to use your words to tell me where it itches!"

"Oh, I thought you knew!" he exclaimed.

"Should I scratch lower or higher?" I asked.

"A little higher, Mom. Oh, that feels so good!"

Later that week, I found myself playing out a rerun of this scene with my husband, after meeting him for a barbecue at the home of a friend.

"Linda," he said, "you know it really bothers me for you to be late to parties."

"I didn't know that bothered you," I said.

He cocked one eyebrow. "We've been married for fourteen years. How could you not know?"

I laughed. "Even after all these years, I still can't read your mind. You still have to use your words to tell me."

Paul raised both brows and grinned. "I don't like for you to be late. Got it?"

I nodded. "Thanks for letting me know! I'll try to do better, OK?"

As I thought about the conversations I'd had with the two men in my life, I wondered how many times I'd miscommunicated by using assumptions instead of words.

Do my own presuppositions cause me to miss what God wants to communicate to me? I wondered.

I remembered how I had assumed that God would heal my daughter. After all, when my nineteen-year-old brother, Jimmy, had been hit by a drunk driver, the doctors had said that Jimmy was paralyzed and would never walk again.

Yet one year after the accident, my brother did walk. A few years later, he even walked down the aisle with his beautiful bride.

But seven years after Laura's accident, I was surprised to find she was still wheelchair bound.

Yet God has shown me that my preconceptions for what He had planned for Laura had been incorrect. Over time, He lovingly communicated how, even though He had not authored her tragedy, He used it for good. Paul said in Romans 8:28,

> "We know that in all things God works
> for the good of those who love him,
> who have been called according to his purpose."

God has shown me that despite my original assumptions, He is still at work—in ways I can't even presume to know.

As I am learning not to presume His plans, I am also learning to share my own thoughts and dreams with Him. This—along with regular prayer and Bible reading—helps make for better communication. And when I follow this communication principle, He helps me scratch that itch. And that feels oh, so good!

Milestones

31

"Is today tomorrow yet?" my son asked me when he was five years old.

"Well, today is yesterday's tomorrow," I volunteered. "It's also tomorrow's yesterday."

Jimmy looked puzzled at this dizzying thought. After all, life is a blur of tomorrows that have become yesterdays, each filled with important milestones. But when it comes to my kids, these milestones can wake me with shock when one phase of their lives turns into another.

Jimmy's greatest milestone came on his sixth birthday—a day he had dreamed of all year.

"Mom, I want a pizza party!" he announced six months

before his big day.

Three months later, he traded this dream party for another. "I want my party at the kids' play center with all my friends!"

Finally, a month before his birthday, he hit upon his final idea. "Mom, please, please, please, give me a surprise party!"

As the days drew closer to December 8, Jimmy would often advise, "Don't tell me you're giving me a surprise party. It's a secret! OK?"

"OK," I answered, unsure of how to handle this dilemma.

"Guess what?" he'd tell a stranger in line with us at the grocery store. "I'm having a surprise birthday party!"

What was I to do? How could I truly give Jimmy a surprise party when he knew not only the days, but the minutes, till his birthday?

I'll surprise him by throwing his party a day early! I decided.

Everyone cooperated. My friend Mickie kept him busy at her farm while I decorated the living room with streamers, set clown paper plates around the table, and made the pink lemonade.

Fifteen minutes before the party, the guests and a colorful clown arrived. Eleven kids hid behind the Christmas tree and living-room furniture, waiting for the big moment.

We practiced our cue while we waited. "When you hear me say, 'Look at the Christmas tree,' jump from your hiding places and shout 'Surprise!'" I explained. After a few practices and several false starts, we were ready.

Mickie's car finally pulled into our driveway. I peeked through the shutters and watched as my bundled-up son, followed by Mickie's kids, skipped to the front door.

When Jimmy came inside, he clutched an "unsuspected" birthday present, wrapped in red Christmas paper, and said, "Look what Mickie gave me to put under our tree!"

As I ushered my son around the corner, I said, "Jimmy, look at the Christmas tree!"

On cue, the children jumped from their places. "Surprise!"

I giggled as Jimmy's face registered shock! He stared at his friends, then ran from the room! I found him in his bedroom, changed into a fresh shirt and combing his hair!

The recognition of the milestone flashed. And I knew the days of the terrible twos were gone forever. My not-long-ago preschooler had changed into a mature kindergartner.

My discovery was bittersweet. I'll so miss that chubby-cheeked child who, despite his many tantrums, gave me so much joy. But you know, I'd much rather Jimmy continue on his journey to adulthood than freeze-frame in the present.

The Bible says in 1 Corinthians 13:11:

"When I was a child, I talked like a child,
I thought like a child, I reasoned like a child.
When I became a man, I put childish ways behind me."

Maybe that means there comes a time when I should change into a fresh shirt and comb my hair without being asked. It can be sad to leave one phase of life for another, but it is also exciting. But it is even more exciting because my children and I do not have to pass our milestones alone. We have a heavenly Father who loves us and walks with us every day. He holds our hands, goes before us, and opens

our doors. I'm left with cherished memories of today's soon-
to-be tomorrows and a Father who makes the best traveling
companion in the universe!

32

Close Encounters

"Be careful what you pray for" should have been my instruction to my kids when I was their summer youth director. It would have been, if I had known how dangerous getting what you pray for can be.

"Let's pray for a miracle," I had suggested to the young people at the small southwest Texas church where I worked during my summer break from Lamar University.

"Let's dream up a prayer that seems too big even for God—and let's see what He does with it."

Veronica, a tiny teenager with dark brown hair and eyes to match, raised her hand. "You've been teaching us how to tell people about Jesus," she said. "Let's pray God will give us the chance to witness to our town's gang leaders!"

I gulped, thinking of the tough brown-skinned teens who helped smuggle drugs over the Mexican border for the local crime syndicate.

"All right," I said, "why not? Let's pray we will get a chance to witness to Mundo and Manuel."

The young people bowed their heads and prayed earnestly. But despite our prayer for a miracle, I felt safe. These tough teens we were praying for were not likely to visit our church. And I was not likely to see them on the street. *Although*, I thought, *maybe one of my teens will get a chance to talk to them in the safety of the local market.*

The summer went by fast—full of fun and excitement. We swam in the Frio River, the kids worked hard on their prayer notebooks, and several went to a retreat at a local campground. One week, I was even privileged to get another nineteen-year-old partner, Rachle Silva, to help lead a Vacation Bible School at the Spanish church across town. Our successful week ended with a rousing parents' night. We stood by proudly as our young charges sang and signed "Jesus Loves Me" in American Sign Language.

Afterward, the stars above the west Texas town twinkled in a cloudless sky as Rachle and I waited in the deserted parking lot for the elderly pastor to drive us home.

I noticed two teen boys walking down the road toward the church. As they approached, the street light broke the shadows to reveal their faces. My heart pounded—it couldn't be—the faces belonged to Mundo and Manuel, the teen drug runners my youth group had been praying for.

This could mean trouble, I realized as I watched the boys

advance. I was relieved when they passed us by. But a few minutes later, the boys returned.

I tried to ignore them.

"Hey, Linda!" a drunken voice called out.

Goose bumps crawled up my arms. *Bad sign. They've been drinking, and they know my name—even though we've never been introduced!*

"What do you want?" I called into the darkness.

"Come over here!"

Rachle shouted back, "No, you come over here."

The two young men approached. Even under the dimness of the street light, I could see hate filling their bloodshot eyes. "What do you want?" I called again, trying to sound calm.

Manuel stepped forward, crowding me with his alcoholic breath. I stepped back, trying to escape the fumes.

"What do we want?" Manuel slurred. "We want you to prove that God is real!"

I swallowed hard. "God loves you. His Son died for the things you've done wrong. In fact, John 3:16 says,

'God so loved the world, that he gave his only begotten Son, that whosoever believeth in him should not perish, but have everlasting life' [KJV].

If you ask Him, He will forgive you and will be a part of your life."

"I don't want you to tell me about God. I want you to prove to me that He is real," Manuel replied, stepping even closer.

"I can prove it only by telling you He is in my heart."

Manuel towered over me, his voice cold and threatening. "That's not good enough. We want you to prove there is a God, and we want you to prove it *now!*"

As Manuel had encroached into my space, I backed into a wall. Now I could back up no farther. I glanced around nervously. *There's nowhere to run and no one to help!*

Lord, I prayed, *there is nothing more I can say to these young men to prove You are real. Would You please take over now? It's up to You.*

As I finished my silent prayer, the beautiful starry night changed. A strong wind rose, swirling sand that pelted our faces. High above our heads, a cloud blotted out the stars as it broke the blackness with jagged streaks of lightning.

Everyone froze while the wind whipped our hair and blinded our eyes. Rachle shouted above the booms of thunder, "See, that is God telling you He is real!"

No one argued.

The frightened boys ran one way, and Rachle and I ran the other. A few minutes later, the cloud passed and calm returned. When Rachle and I reached the home where we were staying, we were still awed. We sat on our bed in the safety of our little bedroom and smiled at each other.

"You know," I said, repeating myself for the hundredth time, "that really was God. He really was there."

"Yes," Rachle agreed, nodding as if in a trance. "He was awesome!"

The excitement of our discovery gave us a sleepless but joyful night. And I learned that God can reveal Himself—not only to two naive college women, but also to two teen smugglers who dared to ask for proof of His existence.

I've also learned to be careful about what I pray for—careful to pray for whatever impossible dream He may put into my heart. After all, I never know what miracles God may perform unless I dare to ask.

The Big Birthday Cry

Have you ever wondered what it would be like if you lacked the ability to communicate?

Although nine-year-old Laura cannot talk, she often communicates through a series of tongue and face signals. She can also nod her head by chewing. Her smiles and frowns help her communicate to her world.

For example, through her signals, she recently let her tutor know that she could count up to nine—a skill we had not known she possessed.

After hearing the good news, I gave Laura a hug. "Boy, Laura, you are one smart kid!" I said.

Laura frowned, then stuck out her tongue in her pointed

No signal!

"Yes, you are!" I said. "I know you cannot always tell us what you are thinking, but that doesn't mean you are not smart. You are very smart."

Laura responded by showing me her "happy tongue," which she wagged down her chin.

Several days later, at her brother's surprise birthday party, Laura was the most excited child in the room. All smiles, she couldn't wait to surprise Jimmy!

During the party, she was thrilled to get a sack of party favors. With alert eyes, she watched a former circus clown juggle red balls before making silver quarters disappear into thin air. When the clown twisted a yellow balloon into the shape of a dog and handed it to her, she laughed silently. She was happier still when the clown painted a pink heart on her cheek.

While the other kids ate birthday cake, Laura licked icing off her spoon. Her eyes sparkled as she tasted her cold vanilla ice cream.

Finally, Laura grew tired and closed her eyes to tell her nurse she was ready to go back to her bedroom.

Later, as she lay in her bed, she began to sob. I went to her room to try to understand what had upset her. "Did something bad happen to you at the birthday party?" I asked.

Tears filled Laura's eyes as she gave me her Yes tongue signal.

"Did someone upset you?" I asked, stroking her dark, silky hair.

When Laura closed her eyes, I knew I was not on the right track.

"Are you upset because you did not get a birthday present?" I asked, desperate to make sense of her tears. Finally, I got a nod!

I ran to my secret Christmas-gift stash and pulled out a videotape I had planned to give her on Christmas morning. Then I hurried back to her room. "Here's a present for you!" I told her, hoping to brighten her mood.

Still, Laura grieved. As I looked at her red face and puffy eyes, I wanted to cry too. I just couldn't understand what it was she was trying so hard to tell me. Laura cried herself to sleep that night, exhausted. I felt exhausted too. If only I could understand why she was so unhappy.

The next day, Laura was no better. When I mentioned the situation to my friend Mickie, she asked, "Did Laura get to open her bag of party favors?"

"You know, I don't think she did," I replied thoughtfully.

I marched back to Laura's room. "Laura, are you sad because you didn't get to open your bag full of birthday surprises?"

A grin spread across Laura's face! She gave me her Yes tongue signal and nodded. I hurried to the kitchen, found her bag, and brought it to her.

As we opened it, she cooed with glee. I pulled out a miniature plastic dinosaur egg and held it for her it see. When I opened it, Laura grinned as a plastic baby dinosaur landed on her chest. She smiled as I fastened a pink imitation watch onto her arm. I couldn't help but smile too. I was glad I had finally communicated with my daughter, yet I was sorry it had taken me so long to do so.

When I think about my relationship with God, I realize I sometimes fail to communicate with Him too—usually because I don't tell Him how I feel or ask Him for help. God so wants me to take time to talk with Him. And unlike Laura, I am never silent because of my limitations. When I'm silent, it is because I have forgotten He is there.

Recently, my friend Frankie told me how sad she was that so many of her friends never take the time to talk to God. But Frankie is not one to miss such an opportunity! She rises at 5:00 a.m. and walks with her Lord every morning. As she walks, she enjoys the sunrise and tells God what is on her heart. She speaks to God, and He speaks to her. Maybe not in an audible voice but with a warm love, which gladdens her heart.

Frankie says, "My friendship with God is the most important thing in my life. Yes, I love my husband and kids, but I am so glad the Lord of the universe communicates with me. It's the happiest hour of my day."

I, too, am so glad God hears and receives my prayers. As Psalm 6:9 says,

*"The Lord hath heard my supplication;
the Lord will receive my prayer" (KJV).*

For when I pray, not only do I know God has heard me; I know He is always open to receiving whatever I say. To know He is always available and will never ignore me makes it easier to come before Him and simply tell Him whatever is on my heart. Whenever I come to Him in prayer, I feel connected with His love. That connection makes all the difference, not only in my day, but in how I handle the pressures of my life.

Memory Quilting

The aroma of roasted turkey still lingered, mixed with whiffs of home-baked rolls and traces of pumpkin pie. Bonnie and I settled into the soft blue-and-rose floral cushions of the living-room sofa. We could hear happy shrieks of my young son and her two children echoing through the house as they played a game of chase. Our husbands were somewhere beneath our feet in Paul's basement office, toying with his computer.

I sighed deeply, content this Thanksgiving Day was at a most peaceful end. Memories of preceding Thanksgivings pieced themselves together in my mind's eye. Some came in pleasant, eye-pleasing patterns. . . . I stared at the small purple wheelchair that stood in the corner. Some memories only darkened the past.

Mentally shelving my remembered grief, I pulled my quilt over my lap and turned to study my friend Bonnie. I thought of our twenty-year friendship that had trailed from the halls of a Texas high school to two Texas universities and finally landed in nearby Colorado towns.

"Linda," Bonnie confided in hushed tones, breaking through my daydreams, "I have something I want to tell you. Something I haven't told anyone else."

"What's that?" I asked, stifling a yawn.

Bonnie said, "Steve and I are getting a divorce."

The news snipped remnants of time into layered patches. Fifteen years unraveled, and I remembered a much younger Steve. A Steve who came bounding across the university campus to where Paul, then my boyfriend, and I sat on a green carpet of grass beneath a shady oak.

"I have the most wonderful news," Steve said with a grin. "We're going to get married!"

"Who is it? I asked, standing.

"Bonnie Loran," he announced.

"Bonnie!" I gave him a hug. "I'm so happy for you!"

Later, when Paul and I were newlyweds, enrolled in a north Texas graduate school, Steve and Bonnie lived a few blocks away. We often celebrated holidays with husband-blackened barbecues in the park.

Steve and Bonnie had then followed us to Colorado, relocating in nearby Greeley. Bonnie had dropped out of school to take care of two-year-apart babies while Steve studied for his doctorate. The love was thick in their tiny trailer despite the dresser-drawer nursery and the master bedroom on a fold-out couch.

I remembered how Steve and Bonnie had been there for Paul and me when tragedy had struck our lives.

I blinked hard and reached for Bonnie, who had slumped into the cushions. "What happened?" I asked, grief-stricken.

"Steve is dating one of my best friends."

The impact of Steve's betrayal tossed my own dreams into nightmares. The ripping apart of the fabric of Bonnie's life seemed to rend my own. In a recurring nightmare, I dreamed Paul would announce he had a new girlfriend and I had to move out of our home. I became cross with Paul, snapping at him at the slightest provocation.

My nighttime nightmares were compounded by real life. Bonnie and the kids moved in with us for two weeks while she tried to decide what to do.

Later, she said, "Steve's betrayal has been more devastating than if he had died. In one blow, I've lost my in-laws, my friends, and my church. It's like my whole life—memories included—has been devoured by a tornado."

I felt as if I was in a tornado, too, as four more dear friends plunged into the divorce process.

One evening, Paul and I sat down together. "Why have you been so upset lately?" he asked.

"I'm sorry," I said. "All these divorces are really getting to me. I can't help but recall the happy times we spent together. Now, we will never be able to share time with these couples again."

Paul sighed. "It's really sad, isn't it?"

I nodded my agreement. "I just don't understand why our

friends want to throw away their past."

Later, this question haunted my thoughts as I picked through another couple's nineteen years worth of discarded accumulation.

"I don't want any of it," Vicki had said. "I have a new life now, a new love. All this old stuff just reminds me of Bill, and I don't want to think of him anymore. You can take whatever you want."

As I sifted through Vicki's things, I realized how many of Vicki's memories were my memories. I silently grieved for this loss as I folded the ivory embroidered tablecloth she and Bill had bought in Mexico.

I stroked the decorative pillows Vicki herself had crafted for their home, remembering the love that had gone into the tiny stitches. Upon seeing her seafoam green quilt, I remembered how excited Vicki had been when she used it to decorate their bedroom. And now, these things, these memories, meant nothing to her. The gracefulness of the Dresden plate quilt that had once covered her marriage bed seemed to mock me. How, I wondered, could Vicki walk away from nineteen years of marriage to a loving husband? How could she exchange her past for a stranger?

Sifting through Vicki's memories was troubling. But more troubling was when I began sifting through my own memories.

Again, I thought of the pain of our family's tragedy, and I remembered how I had almost allowed grief to destroy the pattern of my own life's quilt. . . .

It had been Paul's and my first chance to get away from the intensive-care unit that had invaded our home following

Laura's car accident. That evening, as we sat in an open-air restaurant, Paul asked, "Would you have married me if you had known our daughter would be so severely disabled?"

I felt the night breeze rearrange my curls as I thought through the events of our recent past. I thought of the ten months that Laura had spent in a coma. I thought of all the emotional suffering that had stitched itself into a shroud of grief. I thought of Laura's wheelchair and life-support systems. "No," I finally whispered, willing to throw away the past in exchange for relief from my pain.

Paul stared at his plate, unable to look at me.

"I'm sorry," I said. "I love you, but I would have done anything to prevent Laura from being hurt, even if that meant never meeting you."

But now, five years later, as I looked at the remains of Vicki's discarded memories, I changed my mind about my answer to Paul's question. My memories, even the painful ones, were now precious to me.

Other memories began playing through my mind like bright ribbons of color—I remembered the early-marriage water fights we'd splashed through our tiny lime green apartment. I thought of the day Paul had almost squeezed off my fingers as I birthed our son. I thought about how hard Paul had worked to build our cedar fence so baby Laura and then Jimmy could toddle about the backyard of our first home.

Yes, some of our memories were dark. But as I evaluated them, I realized how even they enriched the quilted pattern they helped to create.

Later that night, I reached for Paul's hand as we sat together on the sofa. "I've changed my mind. I'm sorry I told you several years ago that I wouldn't have married you if I had known our daughter would one day be severely disabled."

Paul's blue eyes met mine, and I squeezed his hand.

"I'm glad I married you. Despite what we've been through, we've been through it together, and I wouldn't change that for anything."

Paul wrapped his arm around my shoulders. "I feel the same way."

"It's too bad about our friends," I added.

Paul said, "When midlife questions caused them to evaluate their lives, they threw out the most valuable possession they shared—each other."

"And their memories," I added.

"It's a waste," Paul concluded. "Keeping their past could have helped ensure their future."

I snuggled closer to my husband, glad I had someone committed to making heirloom memories with me as long as the Lord would allow. And despite all our obstacles, we not only had each other, we also had God—and we would overcome. For 1 John 5:4 says,

"Everyone born of God overcomes the world."

And with things in fresher perspective, I would cherish every patchworked moment of the crazy quilt that had become our lives.

To contact Linda regarding speaking engagements
write her at
PO Box 7562
Longmont, CO 80501

or

e-mail her at
LSwrites @ aol.com

How can one Bible passage possibly Change a person's life Forever?

True stories of people whose lives were changed by a single scripture

Ron & Dorothy Watts

What happens when a person stumbles upon that "moment of trut[h] when the written Word becomes the changing living Word? Can the Bibl[e] possibly pack so much power that its words can transform darkness into li[ght] non believers into believers? Powerf[ul] Passages recounts the incredible and inspirational true stories of remarkab[le] Christians throughout history whose pivotal moments in life were their di[rect] encounters with specific Bible passa[ges]. After reading each story, you'll want [to] share them with others. Use them to enhance family worships, provide to[pics] of discussion for prayer groups, or s[hare] with shut-ins to brighten their day.

Catalog Number 0164240
ISBN # 0-8163-1337-7
192 pages, paper
US$10.99/Cdn$15.99
(prices subject to change)

©1996 Pacific Press Publishing Association175/80700